Are you ready to learn about animals? Your education begins with CHEETAH®. Are you ready? Let's go! Let's go!

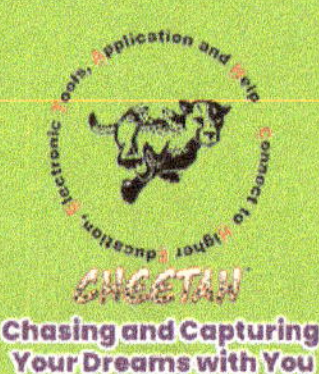

My A to Z Animal Nursery Rhymes

My A to Z Animal Nursery Rhymes

My A to Z Animal Nursery Rhymes

My A to Z Animal Nursery Rhymes

ox

pig

quoll

umbrella
bird

vulture

yellow–eyed
Penguin

zebra

10 9 8 7 6 5 4 3 2 1

First published 2022 with a non-exclusive licence from the authors to **CHEETAH™ Purrrrrrr Publishing**, an imprint of **CHEETAH™ Toys & More, LLC (CHEETAH®)**.

ISBN-13: 979-8-3303-9329-9

Contact information:
CHEETAH™ Toys & More, LLC.
207 Main Street, 4th Floor
Hartford, CT 06016

Port Antonio P.O.
Portland, Jamaica
info@mycheetahinc.com
paulettetrowers@yahoo.com
876-909-6311 (WHATSAPP ONLY)

Authors: Paulette Trowers, Juris Doctor and Steven Doyle
Chief editor: Fiona Porter-Lawson
Illustrator: Rohit Shrivastava and his team

This book belongs to:

____

gifted by:

____

on:

____

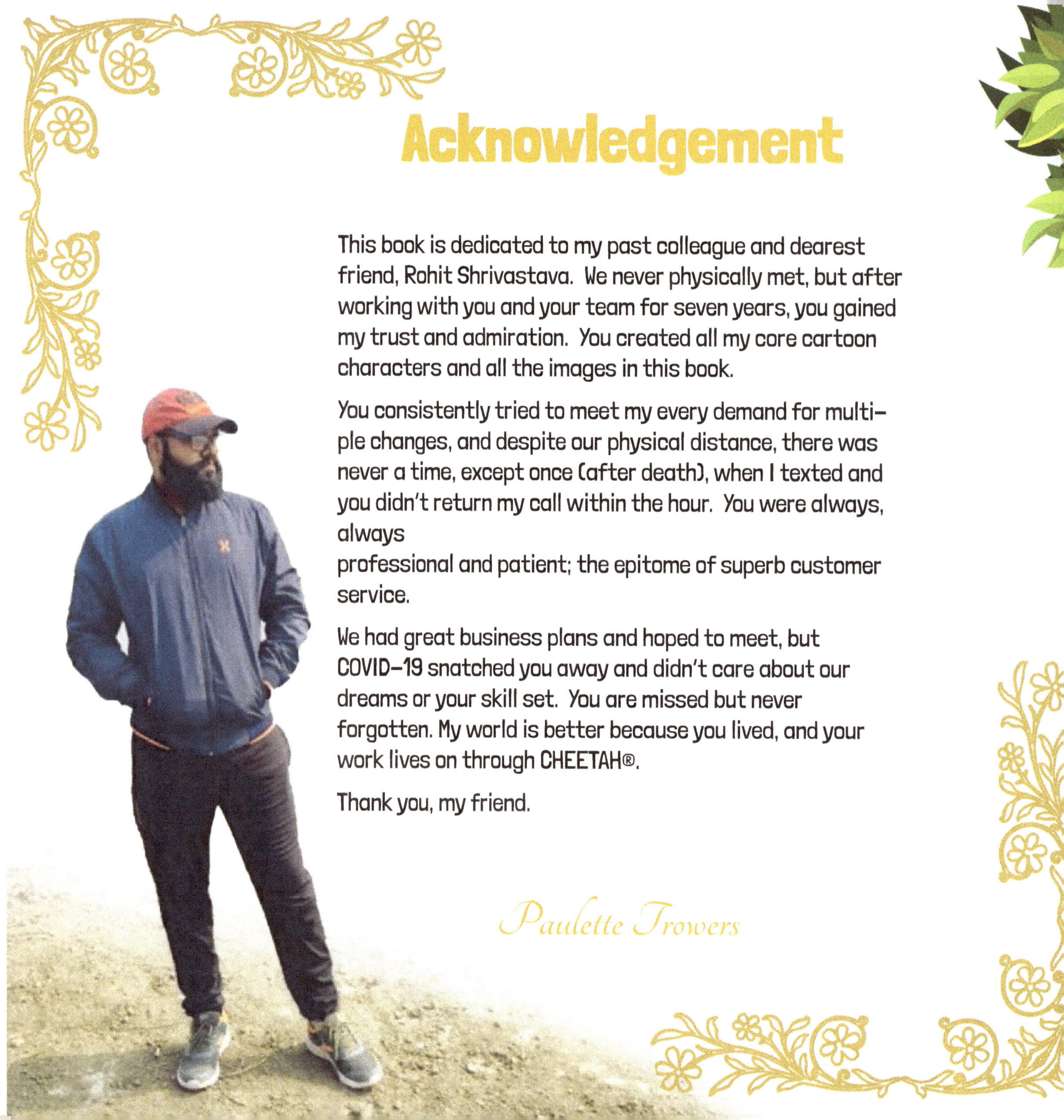

Acknowledgement

This book is dedicated to my past colleague and dearest friend, Rohit Shrivastava. We never physically met, but after working with you and your team for seven years, you gained my trust and admiration. You created all my core cartoon characters and all the images in this book.

You consistently tried to meet my every demand for multiple changes, and despite our physical distance, there was never a time, except once (after death), when I texted and you didn't return my call within the hour. You were always, always
professional and patient; the epitome of superb customer service.

We had great business plans and hoped to meet, but COVID-19 snatched you away and didn't care about our dreams or your skill set. You are missed but never forgotten. My world is better because you lived, and your work lives on through CHEETAH®.

Thank you, my friend.

Paulette Trowers

ABOUT THIS BOOK

CHEETAH TALES: My A to Z Animal Nursery Rhymes

Are you a parent or teacher looking for the perfect addition to a school curriculum?

Look no further. Brought to you by **CHEETAH**™ (**C**onnect to **H**igher **E**ducation, **E**lectronic **T**ools, **A**pps & **H**elp), this is a bundled educational package; a **CHEETAH**™ Treasure Trove.   These poems are for infants, toddlers and school-age children. They will learn about animals with names starting from letters A to Z, the world around them, shapes, colours, and more. The rhyming poems are laid out simply with vivid descriptions and some humour thrown in too.

Along with the short nursery rhymes, children will love the fun facts, posters, playing cards, and activities. If you don't want to read, or if the child in your life cannot read yet, then there are our audio files included for each poem too with awesome sound effects.

This book is designed to help children learn and play and is packed with fun and educational content that promotes critical thinking and a sense of wonder about the world around us. If you want to introduce new words, build vocabulary, and share
ideas with children without the pressure of memorising facts, words and numbers, then this set of tools is ideal.

Learning has never been so much fun. Grab this **CHEETAH**™ treasure trove today!

Aa is for ant

Amber, the ant, was walking one day,

when down fell a leaf that blocked her way.

She could not get home
because of that leaf,

but ants are tough and
strong beyond belief.

Amber bent down and used
all her might.

She flung the leaf and got
home before night.

Fun fact: ant

Ants are small but very strong. Most ants are black, brown or red. They have six legs, two stomachs and no ears. What would you do with no ears?

Bb is for bear

There once was a bear
with fur that was blue.

Most bears are brown,
black, and white too.

But Billy, the bear,
was blue as could be,

and instead of the land,
he lived in the sea.

13

Soon Billy woke up.
It had all been a dream.

Billy was brown
with patches of cream.

14

Fun fact: bear

15

Bears are very big and heavy. When it gets cold, they hide in dens, caves and hollow trees. Bears can smell, hear and see much better than we can. Bears make a loud sound called a growl or a roar. Can you roar like a bear?

Cc is for cat

The cat lay down
on the mat for a nap,
and when he woke up,
he looked at his map.

He had plotted the places
of all the mice holes.

Oh, the life of those mice,
the little poor souls.

20

When feeling happy,
the cat likes to play,

and chases mice in circles,
the rest of the day.

Fun fact: cat

Some cats are pets. Other cats are wild and do not make good pets. Cats eat small animals such as mice and lizards. Cats sleep a lot. They can bend and stretch easily. Can you stretch like a cat?

Dd is for dog

As Dilly, the dog,
was almost sleeping,
he heard the sound of
burglars creeping.

All of his people were in bed
for the night,
and he did not want them
to get a fright.

He barked and barked.
He was so loud.
29

He scared the burglars
and felt very proud.

Fun fact: dog

There are many types of dogs. Some live with families as pets. Others live outside. A young dog is called a puppy. Puppies cannot see or hear when they are born. They also do not have teeth.

As they grow, they learn to hear and smell very well. Some dogs are given jobs such as working with the police and people who are blind. The sound a dog makes is called a bark. Do you have a pet dog at home?

Ee is for elephant

Eight elephants stood
straight in a line,

eating green grass they felt
just fine.

They wanted to play
a football game.

So, they called for more
players, and soon they came.

Then eleven elephants
lined up to play.

They kicked the ball
and played all day.

38

Fun fact: elephant

Elephants are the largest land animals. In some countries, elephants are used as transportation and often carry people and heavy loads. A baby elephant is called a calf. Elephants have four legs, long trunks and really big ears.

They use their trunk to suck up water to drink. Elephants are good at remembering things. Can you remember things as well as an elephant?

Ff is for ferret

Fenton, the ferret, is as curious as can be.

He hops through the grass and into a hole he can see.

And down that hole, he finds a bunny,
who tells a joke that is very funny.

43

The bunny and Fenton have fun all day.
With running and chasing and games to
play.
46

Fun fact: ferret

*I*n the wild, ferrets live in tunnels and among tall grass. They are also used as pets. They are very intelligent and can be trained to sit, use a litter box, walk on a leash and shake hands. They are hard workers and love to dance. Their great sense of hearing and smell are better than humans and dogs. However, they have poor eyesight. They are born blind and are so small, they can fit into a teaspoon at birth. Can you tell me fun facts about yourself?

Gg is for goat

50

Gary, the goat, eats the grass that's green.

He loves to think of kings and queens.

Someday he wants to rule
all the farms

and protect the animals
from danger and harm.

But before he gets
his golden crown,

he would just eat grass
and wander around.

Fun fact: goat

Goats live outside in fields or pens.
They eat grass. The sound a goat makes
is called a bleat. A baby goat is called a
kid. Goats can become sad when they are
alone. Do you like to be alone?

Hh is for horse

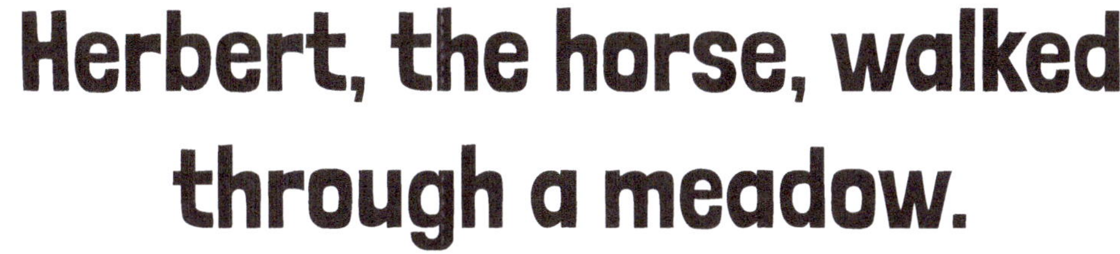

Herbert, the horse, walked
through a meadow.

He saw some bees
who all said hello.

They invited him back to
their home

where they made runny
honey from their
honeycomb.

61

These were special houses,
golden and gummy.

The horse had a lick
and found they were yummy.

Fun fact: horse

65

Horses are big, strong animals. People use them for transportation and fun. They run very fast. A baby horse is called a foal. The sound horses make is called a neigh. Horses have eyes on the sides of their head. They can sleep lying down or standing up. How do you sleep?

Ii is for iguana

Indigo is an iguana,
and his favourite fruit
is a yellow banana.

All day long,
he climbs up trees,

and brings them down
in groups of three.

He sniffs them first
then takes off the peel.

He eats bananas
for every meal.

Fun fact: iguana

The iguana is from the lizard family. It mostly lives in trees. Iguanas have sharp teeth and long toes. They also have sharp tails. They can remove their tails from their bodies if they want to. This is because they can grow new tails. Could an iguana be a pet?

Jj is for jaguar
75

In a faraway jungle
washed over with rain,

there lives a jaguar
by the name of Jane.

She loves her body,
all speckled with spots.

Lots and lots
and lots of dots.

She goes really fast
in joyful run,

and she outraces the rain,
just for fun.

Fun fact: jaguar

Jaguars are part of the big cat family. Most have orange fur with black spots. But some are so black it is hard to see their spots. A young Jaguar is called a cub. Cubs are born with their eyes closed. Their eyes open when they begin to grow. The sound Jaguars make is called a saw. They like to sleep in trees. Can you sleep in a tree?

Kk is for kangaroo

Kangaroo Kate hopped
to the watering hole,
and there she was met
by a water vole.

To the middle, she travelled,
and then to the other side,
she paddled.

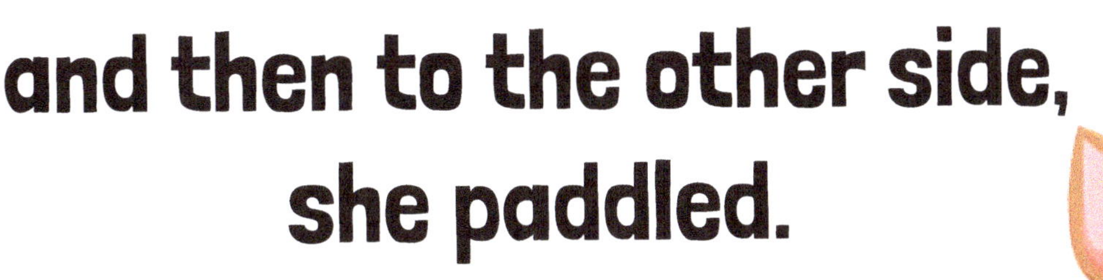

But kangaroos can't swim
in water so deep.

So, she jumped out of the
watering hole in one giant
leap.

Fun fact: kangaroo

$\mathcal{K}$angaroos have very strong legs and big feet. This helps them jump really high. They have a long tail and small ears. Mama kangaroos have a pouch in front to carry their babies. A baby kangaroo is called a joey. It stays in its mother's pouch for a long time. Would you like your mother to carry you in a pouch?

Ll is for lion

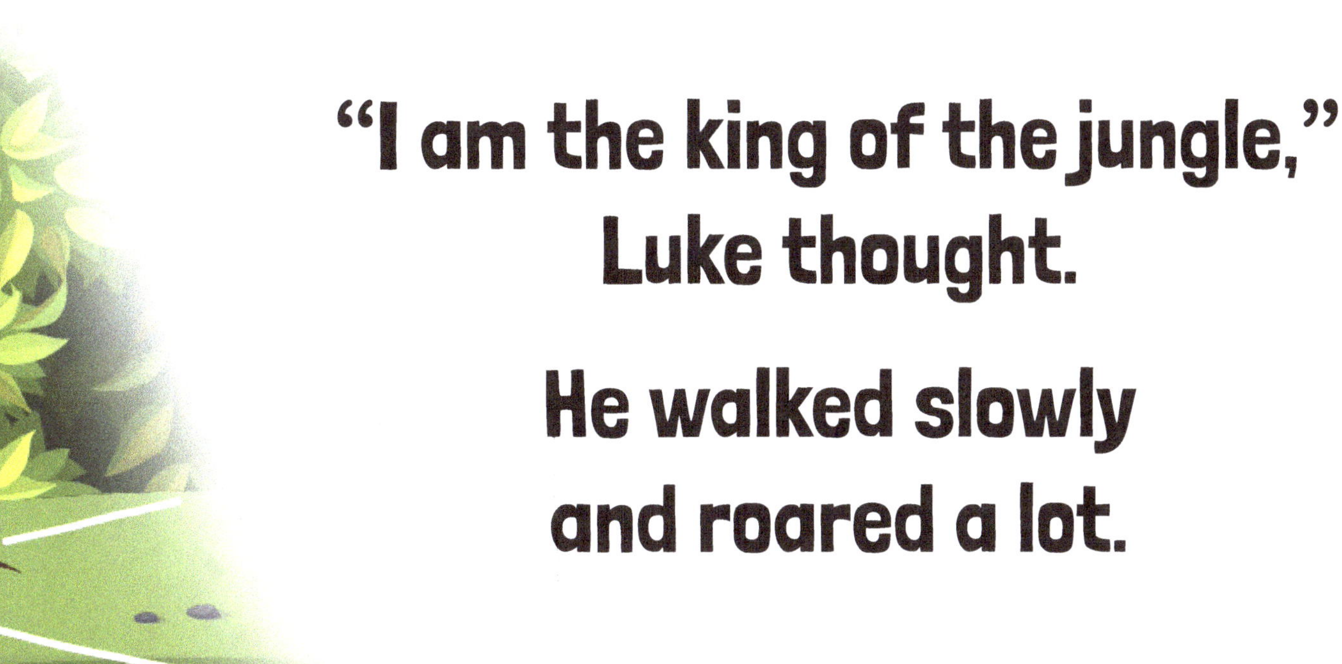

"I am the king of the jungle,"
Luke thought.

He walked slowly
and roared a lot.

93

But as King
he worked all the while.

So, he laid down his crown
with a laugh and a smile.

94

That's when Luke's long reign came to an end.

Instead of being a king, he played with his friends.

Fun fact: lion

Lions are big cats. They live in groups. The baby lion is called a cub. Male lions have thick fur around their heads. The sound they make is called a roar. You can hear a lion roar from very far away. Have you ever seen a lion?

M m is for monkey

On a very big island,
a monkey was stuck.

Mimi, the pirate,
had run out of luck.

Wooden
raft

Under a palm tree
in the light of the moon,

she made a plan
to leave really soon.

This monkey pirate
was a master of craft

and soon escaped
on a rickety raft.

103

Fun fact: monkey

There are many types of monkeys in the world. Monkeys are smart animals. Some can learn numbers and count. The sound that a monkey makes is called a screech or chatter. The baby monkey is called an infant. Some monkeys can run very fast. They like to climb and swing from branches. Do you like to climb?

Nn is for newt

Newton, the newt,
likes to tell the tale

of being chased through
a field by a nightingale.

The bird tried to get at his
nose and his neck.

He tried to cover his nose as
the bird tried to peck.

110

The bird nipped off his tail,
but Newt did not care.

Because newts grow tails
back with fabulous flair.

Fun fact: newt

Newts look a lot like lizards. They have four legs and a long tail. Some live in water but others must live on land. They can grow new legs, eyes or heart. What happens if you lose your legs, hands or eyes?

Oo is for ox

Ollie, the ox, pulled
his orange-filled cart

through bumpy streets.
But deep in his heart
he wished for more.

He wanted
something fresh and fun.

Through hard work,
under the hot, hot sun,

his farmer saved
and was very smart
119

and bought a brand
new octagon cart.
122

Fun fact: ox

An ox has two large horns and one big hump in its shoulders. It is a big, heavy, strong animal. People use them to pull carts and to do work on farms. How strong are you?

P p is for pig

Peggy, the pink pig, looked
like all other pigs.

But this pig had dreams,
which were very big.

This pink pig wanted
to be unique.

So, she went down
by the rippling creek.

She rolled all through
a pile of blueberries

and became the pig
who was purply-blue.

Fun fact: pig

Pigs are smart animals. They can be trained just like dogs. A pig's nose is called a snout. They use their snout to dig dirt and smell food. A baby pig is called a piglet. The mother pig sometimes sings to the piglets when she is feeding them. Do you like when someone sings to you?

Qq is for quoll
133

The quoll came quietly when
the moon was high,
and saw a big ball of white
up, up in the sky.

135

He quickly climbed up the
tallest of trees

and was sure that the moon
was made of cheese.

But it was not cheese
when he took a big bite.
A quoll is eating the moon.
Oh, what a sight.

Fun fact: quoll

Quolls have brown or black fur and a pink nose. They eat plants, small birds and insects. They like to climb. The sound they make is called a bark or growl. Their babies are called joeys. Do you know an animal with a pink nose?

140

R r is for rabbit

141

Rosy, the rabbit,
was looking for food,

when a rooster came by
in a really good mood.

"I will help you find some food," the rooster said.

"I know a field where carrots are spread."

143

145

The rooster flapped,
and the rabbit hopped,

and together they rushed
to the carrot crop.

Fun fact: rabbit

$\mathcal{R}$abbits hop to move from place to place. They live in tunnels they dig in the ground. They have long ears. A baby rabbit is called a kit. Rabbits' teeth never stop growing, but their teeth get smaller when they eat grass and vegetables. What if your teeth never stopped growing?

Ss is for sheep

Sammy, the sheep,
could not sleep.

So tired he was, that he
started to weep.

151

He looked up above and counted the stars.

He counted them even though they were far.

He counted the silver stars
up in the skies,
and when he counted seven,
he closed his eyes.
153

Fun fact: sheep

A sheep's skin is covered with fleece. Fleece keeps sheep warm. A baby sheep is called a lamb. Sheep can see behind them without turning their heads. Can you do that?

Tt is for tiger

Two tigers stood and stared
at each other.
Timmy was one, the other
his brother.

Between them, they made
two lines, long and straight.

If only there was something
else to create.

Along came their sister and
a triangle was made.
Three tigers together;
for a long time they played.

Fun fact: tiger

Tigers are big wildcats with stripes on their fur and skin. They are the biggest cats in the world. They are very strong and can run very fast. This makes it easy for them to catch other animals. A baby tiger is called a cub. The sound a tiger makes is called a roar.
Do you know how to roar?

Uu is for
umbrella bird

Una sat and groomed her
black feathers.

The top of her head looked
like an umbrella.

For many people,
a storm is a pain,
but the umbrella bird
does not mind the rain.

167

So, Una flapped
and sang her soothing song.

And it did not rain
for very long.

170

Fun fact: umbrellabird

Umbrellabirds live in trees. They hop from branch to branch. They have wings but do not fly very far. These birds have feathers on their heads that look like an umbrella. They have extra skin that hangs from their necks. They look different from other birds. Do you look different from other children?

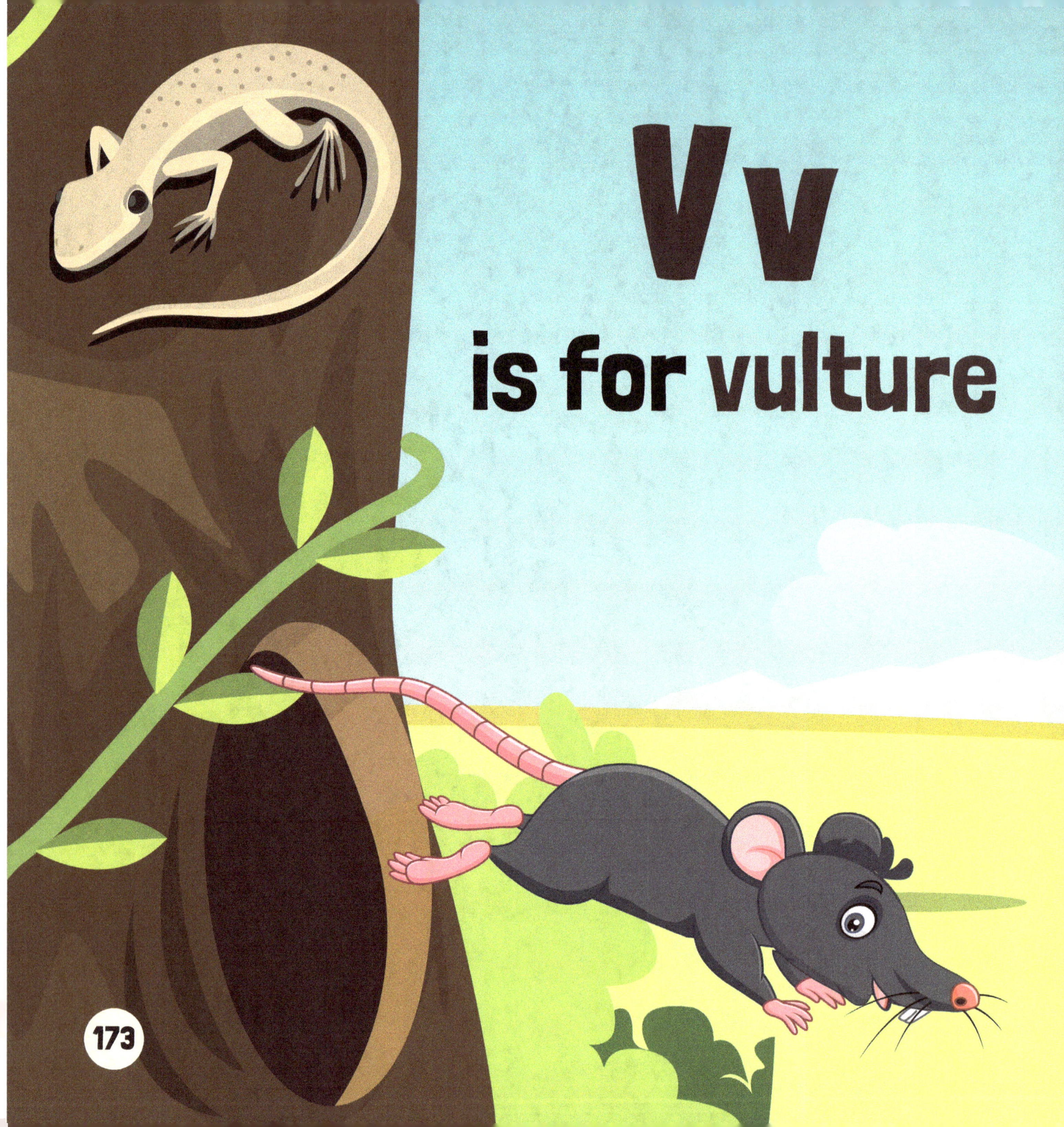
V v
is for vulture
173

A vulture swooped,
looking for food.
A mouse or a lizard
would be very good.

But something caught
his eagle-eyes,

a flash of violet
he spied from up high.

He pounced on the blueberry
and pecked it with his beak.

From that moment on, he
ate fruit every week.

Fun fact: vulture

Vultures are big birds. They live in trees and can fly. They have very large wings but have no feathers on their heads. They can see and smell very well. They eat sick or dead animals. This helps to clean up our world. Have you ever seen one before?

W w is for wolf

The worried wolf wandered
through the snow

lost from his family three
weeks ago.

He was really sad, and
on his face was a scowl.

Then, from a distance
came a hushed howl.

He threw back his head
and made a howl that was loud.

His mother and father had
finally been found.

187

Fun fact: wolf

Wolves are part of the dog family. They have fur to keep them warm. They live in cold places. Wolves can run very fast for a long time. They have sharp teeth and like to eat large animals. A young wolf is called a pup. The sound wolves make is called a howl. Can you make that sound?

Xx is for fox

The fox went running
through the trees.

Chased by hunters;
one, two, three,

four men on horses with
five barking dogs.
The clever fox jumped
over some logs.

193

Then found a stump,
a place to hide.

This fox is smart,
cunning and sly.

Fun fact: fox

$\mathcal{F}$oxes are small and can run very fast. They eat small animals like rabbits, mice and insects. A baby fox is called a pup, kit or cub. The sound that the fox makes is called a bark. A fox makes about fourty different sounds. How many sounds can you make?

Yy is for Yellow-eyed penguin

Yanny walked under the
cloudless blue skies

looking at the view
with bright yellow eyes.

He said hi to the walrus with
long, sharp tusks,

then waved to the whale
who did flips and tucks.

He nodded in greeting to a
yak on a yacht

and bowed to the polar bear,
whom he never forgot.

204

Fun fact: yellow-eyed penguin

Yellow-eyed penguins have grey eyes. As they grow, a yellow band forms around their eyes. They can live for twenty years. They eat food from the ocean such as fish. Do you eat fish?

Zz is for zebra

Zoey, the zebra,
played hide and go seek.

She moved quietly
through the woods.
She did not speak.

She tried her best as she
hid behind a bush so green.

She wanted to vanish
and not be seen.

210

But it can be very,
very hard to hide

with black stripes and white
on each side.

Fun fact : zebra

A zebra is white with black stripes. The stripes on each zebra are different. No two zebras look the same, Zebra babies are called foals. Zebras only have one toe on each foot. How many toes do you have?

Cc is for Cheetah

Comet, the cheetah, wakes
up and grooms her fur.
Then runs really fast—so
fast, she's a blur.

She plays with her brothers
and sisters. What fun!

They explore and hunt until
they are done.

Comet takes a nap when the
day gets too hot.

Then hunts for her dinner
just like she was taught.

Fun fact : Cheetah

Cheetahs are the fastest animals on land and can run faster than some cars! They can't roar like other big cats, but they do like to purr. Cheetahs like to live in groups with other cheetahs. Their fur helps them blend in and not be seen. These large cats are mainly found in Africa, however, they are becoming extinct (not existing anymore). Are you becoming extinct?

223

My A to Z
Animal Poster
CHEETAH
Chasing and Capturing
Your Dreams with You
www.mycheetahinc.com

My Letters of the Alphabet

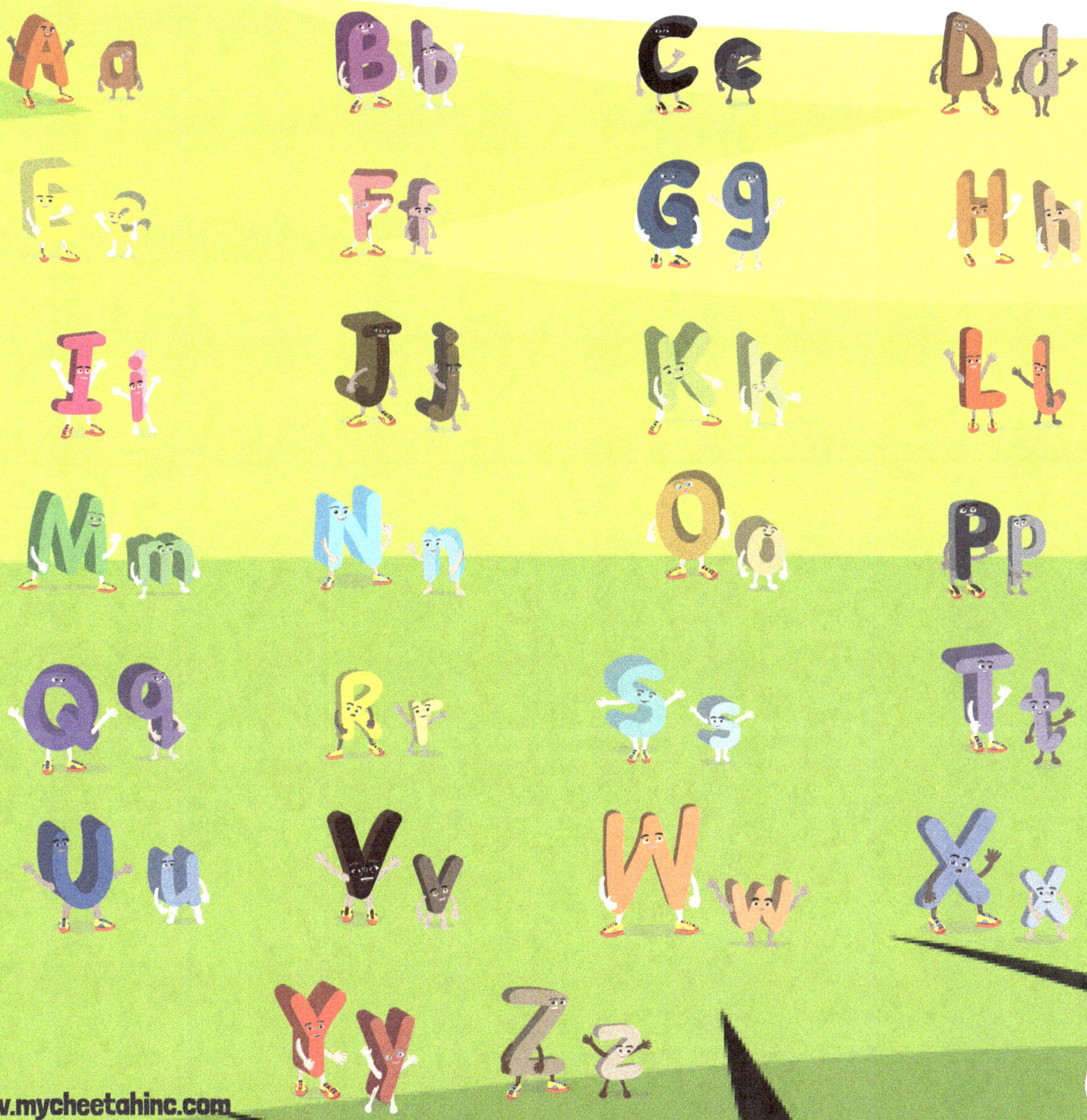

Aa Bb Cc Dd
Ee Ff Gg Hh
Ii Jj Kk Ll
Mm Nn Oo Pp
Qq Rr Ss Tt
Uu Vv Ww Xx
Yy Zz

www.ingramcontent.com/pod-product-compliance
Lightning Source LLC
Chambersburg PA
CBHW060112120726
48003CB00009B/2605